WASHINGTON, D.C.

IN PHOTOGRAPHS

WASHINGTON, D.C.

IN PHOTOGRAPHS

In collaboration with the travel experts at Fodor's

Alexander D. Mitchell IV

GRAMERCY BOOKS
NEW YORK

© 2005 PRC Publishing,
The Chrysalis Building,
Bramley Road, London W10 6SP

An imprint of Chrysalis Books Group plc

This 2005 edition is published by Gramercy Books, an imprint of Random House Value Publishing, a division of Random House, Inc., New York, by arrangement with Chrysalis Books, London.

Gramercy is a registered trademark and the colophon is a trademark of Random House, Inc.

Random House
New York • Toronto • London • Sydney • Auckland
www.randomhouse.com

Printed and bound in China

A catalog record for this title is available from the Library of Congress.

ISBN 0-517-22655-3

10 9 8 7 6 5 4 3 2 1

Credits
Editor: Anne McDowall
Designer: Axis Design
Picture Researcher: Carla Penagos
Production: Alice Reeves
Reproduction: Anorax

Additional captions
Page 1: The Capitol at night
Page 2: The Lincoln Memorial, reflecting pool, and Washington Monument

Picture Acknowledgements

L=Left R=Right C=Center T=Top B= Bottom

© **Alexander D. Mitchell IV:** 80B, 91, 119T, 119B, 122R, 124

© **Chrysalis Image Library/Simon Clay:** 2, 18, 24-25, 38, 39, 67B, 70, 89, 94B, 109T, 110, 111.

© **Royalty-Free/Corbis:** 1, 27T, 36, 48T, 60, 101, 114.

© **Corbis:** © George D. Lepp/CORBIS 17. / © Peter Finger/CORBIS 19B./ © Richard T. Nowitz/CORBIS 20-21./ © Catherine Karnow/CORBIS 29. / © MOLLY RILEY/Reuters/Corbis 31. / © James P. Blair/CORBIS 32-33. / © Richard T. Nowitz/CORBIS 37T. / © Lee Snider/Photo Images/CORBIS 40. / © Michael Freeman/CORBIS 41. / © Richard T. Nowitz/CORBIS 44. / © ART on FILE/CORBIS 47. / © Audrey Gibson/CORBIS 49. / © WILLIAM PHILPOTT/Reuters/Corbis 51. / © James P. Blair/CORBIS 54. / Susan Steinkamp 55. / Scott T. Smith 56B. / © Wally McNamee/CORBIS 61. / Galen Rowell/CORBIS 63. / © Bettmann/CORBIS 67T. / © Lee Snider/Photo Images/CORBIS 68. / © Lee Snider/Photo Images/CORBIS 71. / © Bob Rowan; Progressive Image/CORBIS 77. / © Richard T. Nowitz/CORBIS 81. / © Reuters/CORBIS 92T. / © Bob Rowan; Progressive Image/CORBIS 93. / © LARRY DOWNING/Reuters/Corbis 95. / © Richard T. Nowitz/CORBIS 98T. / © Lee Snider/Photo Images/CORBIS 102T. / © James P. Blair/CORBIS 106. / © James P. Blair/CORBIS 109. / © Richard T. Nowitz/CORBIS 122L. / © Catherine Karnow/CORBIS 123. / © MAPS.com/CORBIS 126.

© **Digital Vision:** 11, 117T.

© **Keith Stanley:** 12, 19T, 22, 23, 27B, 28, 30, 45, 48B, 69, 73T, 73B, 74T, 74B, 75, 78, 79, 80T, 84, 85, 87, 92B, 94T, 98B, 102B, 107B, 110T, 125.

© **Lonely Planet Images:** © Lonely Planet Images/Greg Gawlowski 97. / © Lonely Planet Images/Richard Cummins 99, 103.

© **Photolibrary.com:** 2, 6, 7, 10, 13, 14-15, 24-25, 26, 35, 37B, 39, 42-43, 52, 53, 56T, 57, 58T, 58B, 59, 61, 65, 66, 72, 82-83, 87, 90, 100, 105, 113, 115T, 116, 118, 120-121.

© **Pierson Photography:** © The George Washington Masonic National Memorial all rights reserved, Photography by Arthur W. Pierson 117B.

© **Rex Features** 115B.

Contents

INTRODUCTION

Washington, D.C., is by no means a typical city for the average tourist. Unlike most cities, which are a rich conglomeration of businesses and residents, Washington is fundamentally a "company town", with that company being the United States federal government. The major employer in the city is the government and its various departments, and a great many of the other businesses here are located in the region in order to interact with the government—contractors, lobbyists, service industries, and the like. In addition to being a center for government, however, Washington has become, both by accident and design, a cultural and historical center to the nation, and it is home to a great number of the nation's premier museums, foundations, and institutions.

In contrast with the long histories of such cities as London, Rome, and Tokyo, Washington—or more accurately, the District of Columbia, often abbreviated "D.C."—is a fairly young and fresh city, with relatively few of the constraints of ancient heritage and design so common to the older cities. The city arose to a large degree as a compromise of sorts, as a neutral territory situated to please all of the former colonies' regional factions equally.

The area that now forms the District of Columbia came into existence in 1785 when the new Federal government of the former 13 British colonies, having just won independence from Britain, voted to estab-

▶ **Washington Monument:** *Two of Washington, D.C.'s most popular attractions—the Washington Monument and the cherry blossoms of the Tidal Basin—are seen together in the early spring.*

▼ **Chesapeake & Ohio Canal:** *The water-filled trench and lock in Georgetown survives as a historic vestige of one of the nation's earliest transportation arteries. The canal served as a freight artery to and from the Allegheny Mountains to the west, but was largely replaced by railroads before its closure in the 1920s. The towpath survives as a national park, with the Georgetown stretch flooded for boat rides between April and October.*

lish a new "federal town" as the seat of its national government rather than set up shop in one of the existing cities. From the then-unattractive and mosquito-riddled swamplands lining the Potomac River near Alexandria, Virginia, Pierre Charles L'Enfant, a French architect and engineer who had served with George Washington in the Colonial army during the American Revolution, planned a city of grandiose ambitions. The design encompassed broad boulevards, monumental circles, large open plazas, and grand public buildings—ideas derived largely from cities such as Paris and Versailles.

L'Enfant's plans quickly outstripped the fledgling government's meager resources, however. The British invasion during the War of 1812 disrupted progress

considerably with the torching of the Capitol and White House. L'Enfant's planning also largely failed to take into account the commercial realities common to most cities, such as markets and transportation. It would take post-Civil War prosperity and expanding government for many of his proposals to be realized.

By 1900, however, several decades of unchecked and haphazard economic development had taken the District thoroughly astray from the L'Enfant vision, and in that year the McMillan Committee, appointed by Congress, was charged with bringing order to the chaos. The net result of the 1902 Senate Park Commission Report for Washington was to codify the preservation of Washington's open areas and monumental designs. The timing would be fortunate in the

long term, as it came just as the era of the modern skyscraper was beginning; among the report's recommendations was the capping of the permissible height of future buildings to protect the grandeur of the Capitol and Washington Monument. Among the beneficiaries of the McMillan Committee's work was the National Mall between the Capitol and Washington Monument, which by the turn of the century had become a hodgepodge of railroad tracks, museums, markets, and sheds, later transformed into the wide-open vistas we see today.

More changes to Washington's appearance came about in the early twentieth century as the Federal government began to steadily increase its bureaucracy, growing even more during the Roosevelt "New Deal" of the 1930s. Congress formed the Public Buildings Commission in 1916, which produced the Public Buildings Act of 1928. Among the results of 1930s construction were the Supreme Court Building, the House Office Building, the Jefferson Memorial, and a massive complex of office buildings between Pennsylvania Avenue and the Mall, now known as Federal Triangle. Other projects, such as the construction or upgrading of downtown hotels and business offices, rose independently of the government projects. The Washington National Cathedral, begun in 1907 and completed in 1990, arose in the city's northwest.

In common with much of America, the District saw a substantial shift in demographics after World War II as middle- and upper-class residents defected to the suburbs. This flight was aided in part by the options offered by improved suburban transportation corridors, particularly the highway and Interstate development of the 1950s and 1960s. Later, the construction of the Metro subway system—first opened in 1976 and one of the newest subway systems in the nation—did much to advance the ease of commuting from the suburbs. More than the average urban area, Washington has become an employment hub surrounded by "bedroom community" suburbs and "exburbs," with commuters traveling further and further from the city to reach their desired housing. The residents of the District itself are largely—and sharply—divided between the upper-class residents of premium real estate in such areas as Georgetown and Capitol Hill and the low-income residents of

neighborhoods such as Anacostia. Interstate 495, or the Capital Beltway, which rings the District, became a metaphorical wall between life and government "inside the Beltway" and the rest of America "beyond the Beltway." The remaining urban population of the District suffers from a unique quirk: as a Federal jurisdiction, the District lacks representation in Congress, leading to perennial demands for representation that has even carried over to District license plates being printed with "Taxation Without Representation".

As the District entered the twenty-first century, it faced the problems of most American cities—traffic congestion, crime, a widening gap between rich and poor, etc. It also faced an ongoing redefinition of its role in the changing political and economic environment throughout the nation, as well as indirectly as the center of power in the world's most powerful nation after the fall of the Soviet Union.

Unfortunately for the District and the nation, being the center of so much importance can come at a steep price. Terrorist attacks in 2001 targeted both New York City and Washington, one attack successfully crashing an airliner into the Pentagon. As a result, Washington was forced to rethink its relative openness and light security. At the time of going to press, many of the landmarks shown here have either been placed off limits to the public or are operating under the harshest security restrictions of their existence. The delicate dance between the relative transparency and openness of the nation's landmarks and the need for the protection of both the landmarks and the government within continues and the ramifications will no doubt be felt for years.

However, the casual visitor to the District will still find much to enjoy. In spite of security travails, Washington, D.C., remains both an inspirational and exciting city—few cities in the world can share such diversity and grandeur. Millions of Americans come to Washington to visit "their" city annually, along with many more tourists from other countries. The District is home to many of the world's greatest libraries,

◀ **Washington Metro (Dupont Circle):** *One of the nation's most modern subway systems, the Washington Metro boasts spectacular vaulted ceilings and architecture in its underground stations. The system transports hundreds of thousands of passengers to, from, and about the District and its suburbs on a daily basis.*

◀ **Union Station Interior:** *The Main Hall of Washington Union Station, opened in 1908, was modeled in part after ancient Rome's Baths of Caracalla, with majestic columns and ceilings. The small shopping kiosks visible in the contemporary photograph of the Main and East Halls belie the large rail terminal and shopping mall behind and to the left of the photographer.*

▶ **Night view of the Capitol:** *The spectacular nightly floodlighting of the Capitol serves to highlight not only its symbolic "anchoring" of Pennsylvania Avenue, but also its role as the physical center of the District itself (at least as the District was originally laid out). With the District having a relatively low skyline, the Capitol is visible for miles around in most directions.*

museums, medical research centers, theaters, and art galleries. Washington seemingly has a monument, memorial, or park statue on every major intersection or corner—so many, in fact, that many are starting to call for more restraint upon future memorial planning, lest the National Mall ends up looking like one massive cemetery. The Smithsonian Institution has grown from a single building on the National Mall to a diversified complex of museums that would take any tourist a full week to give them their appropriate due visits.

With so much international traffic in politics, diplomacy, and tourism, the District boasts an endless diversity of restaurants, cultural centers, and people. The effects are now felt well beyond the District's borders, with suburbs such as Rockville, Alexandria, and Vienna taking on more and more of a -

cosmopolitan feel. Even in the more remote suburbs, you can run across a fine Italian restaurant, a brew-pub, a South American chicken take-out outlet, a Korean market, and a sushi bar almost within sight of each other. You can return to the tranquility of nature in Rock Creek Park or the National Arboretum, see a variety of animal species at the National Zoo, or partake in the powerful spectacle of Great Falls' Potomac River rapids—the latter with a kayak, if you are daring enough. And you can marvel at the contrast between old and new in the District's Georgetown and Virginia's "Old Town" section of Alexandria, where commercial strips, modern hotels, and upscale boutiques have melded comfortably with or within colonial-era buildings and historic structures and settings.

◄ Capitol Hill Area:
The area to the east and southeast of the Capitol is richly laden with vintage, well-constructed townhouses, many of which (especially along Pennsylvania Avenue and adjacent blocks) now house a variety of eclectic shops, restaurants, bars, and boutiques. The nearby Eastern Market also serves the residents of this area.

► Smithsonian "Castle": *The National Mall is dominated by the Smithsonian Institution's "Castle", the original museum and office building for the Smithsonian. The Norman-styled red sandstone building was designed by James Renwick Jr. and completed in 1855. Rebuilt after an 1865 fire and remodeled many times over the decades, the building now houses a visitors' center and administrative offices for the Smithsonian.*

► ► The White House: *The modern-day demands of security have sharply reduced the symbolic role of the front lawn of the White House as a public gathering place or park. However, the White House lawn still sees the annual Easter Egg Roll each spring.*

The National Mall

The Mall is the two-mile stretch of open green parkland running east to west between Constitution Avenue to the north and Independence Avenue to the south, with the U.S. Capitol at the east end and the Lincoln Memorial at the west end. The Washington Monument stands at the halfway point.

Though the Mall had its genesis in the original L'Enfant plans for Washington, at various times in its history its grandeur has been severely compromised by neglect or emergency. During the later half of the nineteenth century, railroad and horsecar tracks were laid across the Mall, including rail lines that eventually carried a large portion of freight and passenger traffic between the northern states and the South. The McMillan Plan of 1902 was instrumental in restoring much of the Mall's clean appearance, but even during World War II, thousands of dormitories and temporary government buildings were erected upon the Mall to house an enormous number of workers that flooded the District during the war effort.

Today, however, the Mall is largely an empty parkland open to all, seemingly large enough to land a large plane upon, though encroachment by more and more monuments and museums (most recently the National World War II Memorial) continues to nibble at the open vistas. The largest of the museums of the Smithsonian Institution, including the National Museum of American History, the National Museum of Natural History, and several art galleries, ring the Mall, and large numbers of students and tourists cross and stroll along the Mall throughout the temperate seasons.

The Mall remains a popular gathering point, be it for springtime kite flying, popular Smithsonian-organized festivals, or even an occasional protest or statement gathering, such as the "Million Man March" of 1995. So large have many gatherings become that the National Park Service has ceased providing estimates for crowds at such events—estimates long criticized by participants and opponents eager to exaggerate or downplay the importance of such gatherings.

▶ **The National Mall:** *This vast open plaza stretches as a mile-long "avenue of museums" between the Capitol and the Washington Monument, with additional memorials and parkland between the Washington Monument and Lincoln Memorial. The eastern half has become everything from a parade ground for political rallies to a fairground for the annual Smithsonian Folklife Festival. Kites are a frequent sight above the largely treeless plaza, especially during the annual Smithsonian Kite Festival.*

◀ **Washington Monument:** *Neither the first (Baltimore's was dedicated in 1815) nor the only monument in the region dedicated to the nation's first President, the District's 555-foot-high Washington Monument is no doubt the most famous. Construction was begun in 1848, but money ran out in 1853. The Federal government later apportioned funding to complete the monument. When finished in late 1884, it was a radically different obelisk from the grandiose colonnaded temple that was originally proposed.*

▶ **Freer Gallery of Art:** *Opened in 1923, the Freer Gallery of Art was formed around the collection of Asian art donated by Detroit businessman Charles Lang Freer (1856–1919). Sixteen of the nineteen galleries within are devoted to Asian art, including Chinese paintings, Korean ceramics, Japanese lacquerware, Indian sculpture, and Islamic metalware. The other three galleries display nineteenth- and twentieth-century American artwork.*

◄ **National Gallery of Art, West Building:** *The National Gallery of Art evolved from the philanthropy of financier Andrew W. Mellon, who funded a charitable trust upon his death in 1937. Construction began the same year and the building, designed by John Russell Pope, was dedicated in March 1941. Today it houses a collection of European works from the thirteenth century to the present.*

▶ ▶ **National Gallery of Art, East Building:** *In sharp contrast to the Classical architecture of the original West Building, the East Building of the National Gallery, designed by I.M. Pei and opened in 1978, is of a sleek, contemporary design. It houses modern art by European and American artists. The two buildings are connected by a paved plaza and an underground concourse.*

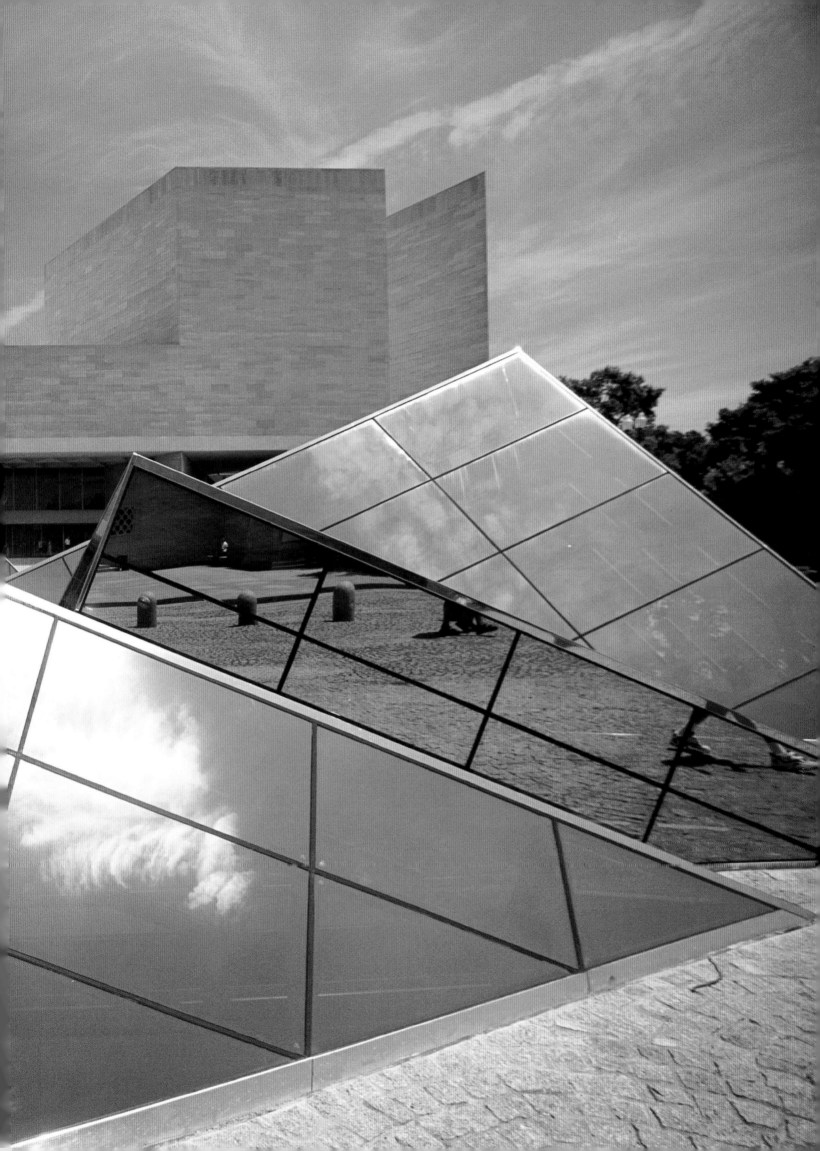

▲ **National Museum of African Art:** *Established in 1987, the National Museum of African Art is a relative newcomer to the Smithsonian "family" of museums. It is dedicated to the exhibition and preservation of the traditional arts and culture of the African continent, primarily the sub-Saharan regions. Like the Sackler Gallery, it is mostly an underground building.*

▶ **National Museum of Natural History:** *One of the oldest of the Smithsonian's museums, the domed Beaux-Arts building now known as the National Museum of Natural History was erected in 1904. Focusing on the natural world, this one branch of the Smithsonian houses more than 85 percent of the Institution's total artifacts, specimens, and items, in the form of animal specimens, mounted insects and leaves, minerals, and fossils.*

▶ **View West toward the Washington Monument:** *A view looking west, beyond the U.S. Capitol, up the National Mall toward the Washington Monument and Lincoln Memorial. Originally planned as a "vast esplanade" by L'Enfant in 1791, the Mall had become a jumble of rail tracks and coal sheds serving a rail station by the late 1800s. Lining the Mall today are many of the museums of the Smithsonian Institution, including the National Air and Space Museum and the Arts and Industries Building.*

▲ **National Archives:** Entrusted with preserving the document history of American government and history, the National Archives is perhaps better known as a shrine housing and displaying the nation's founding documents — the Declaration of Independence, the Constitution, and the Bill of Rights. The temple-like structure was designed by John Russell Pope and erected in 1935 atop the site of a former railroad passenger station.

▶ **Arthur M. Sackler Gallery:** The Freer Gallery is nicely complemented by the adjacent (and mostly subterranean) Arthur M. Sackler Gallery, opened in 1987 and offering the Asian collection of its namesake medical publisher and physician. The permanent collection includes art from China, the Near East, and southern and Southeast Asia; the building also hosts occasional concerts, dance programs, and films.

▲ **Smithsonian "Castle":** *In 1836 the U.S. Congress accepted a bequest of $500,000 from British scientist James Smithson (who, oddly, had never visited the United States) "to found at Washington ... an establishment for the increase and diffusion of knowledge." The result was the Smithsonian Institution, now the world's largest museum and research complex. Nine of its museums are located on the Mall. The red-sandstone Smithsonian Castle, completed in 1855, was the original building for the facility; it now houses Smithsonian offices and a visitors' center.*

◀ **Arts and Industries Building:** *The second-oldest building in the Smithsonian's complex, this brick and sandstone building was erected in 1881 to house items from the nation's 1876 Centennial Exposition in Philadelphia. It then served as the original home of the Smithsonian's National Museum before its massive expansion and subdivision among the many buildings on the Mall.*

▲ **National Air and Space Museum:** *Since its 1976 opening, the museum has been both the city's and the Smithsonian Institution's most popular tourist attraction, with around nine million visitors annually. It covers the history of manned flight and space travel, and includes an early Wright Brothers' prototype plane, Charles Lindbergh's Spirit of St. Louis, and early space flight capsules.*

▲ **Hirshhorn Museum and Sculpture Garden:** Erected in 1974, the Hirshhorn Museum and Sculpture Garden houses a collection of American and European art from the late nineteenth century to date, including mostly paintings and sculpture. To the north of the building lies the Sunken Sculpture Garden, featuring works by, among others, Rodin and Matisse.

▶ **National Museum of the American Indian:** The newest Smithsonian museum on the Mall, opened in September 2004, the National Museum of the American Indian is dedicated to the preservation, history, and study of the historical and contemporary culture of the Native American peoples of the United States and Western Hemisphere. A team of Native American architects designed the building, which is reminiscent of a wind-sculpted mesa.

▷ **National Museum of American History:**

More than any other of the Smithsonian museums, the National Museum of American History is responsible for the Smithsonian's informal role as "the nation's attic." Opened in 1964 as the National Museum of History and Technology, its name was changed in 1980. It houses an amazing diversity of Americana and cultural icons, including the original "Star-Spangled Banner", Alexander Graham Bell's original telephone, props from noted movies and television shows, and a Southern Railway passenger steam locomotive.

Capitol Hill

The term "Capitol Hill" has long not only meant a rise of land upon which America's seat of government sits, but has also become shorthand for the power-brokering activities of the legislative branch of American government that happen upon it. Both the Hill and the expression began to take form not long after the 1787–8 ratification of the United States Constitution. In 1791, a ten-acre plot was ceded by the State of Maryland, and L'Enfant chose the hill—geologically little more than a rise above the riverside flood plain—as the site for the Capitol. Over the next 200 years, the symbolic stature of Capitol Hill and its surrounding neighborhood rose along with the building, and then reached far past it.

The Capitol itself is now surrounded by green landscaping, plazas, and pathways that provide both a physical buffer and an aesthetic grandeur to the building. The area is also home to the Supreme Court, the three main buildings of the Library of Congress, the Congressional office buildings, and the Folger Shakespeare Library.

In the early 1800s, as the fledgling government took form, the area to the east became the site of numerous hotels, boarding houses, tenements, and taverns serving the transitory occupants of Federal government and their associated employees and lobbyists. Many an after-hours deal has been struck in these watering holes. The residential neighborhood to the east is now home to many charming Victorian-era rowhouses, as well as restaurants, shops, offices, and bars, and the wheeling and dealing continues today in the delis, bars, and nightclubs close to the Capitol. The actual Capitol grounds themselves, however, have lately become more fortress-like in character; heavy security barriers and fences exacerbate the already congested traffic and parking situations in the area, with the effects spreading further and further from the Capitol with each successive year.

▶ **U.S. Capitol:** *The physical and symbolic heart of United States government and one of the most recognizable buildings in the world, the United States Capitol has evolved in several stages over the course of many decades, including an expansion in 1959–61, which added 100 additional offices.*

▲ **U.S. Capitol Interior:**

The present cast-iron dome
was erected in the early
1860s to replace a smaller
wooden and copper dome,
part of the original Charles
Bulfinch Capitol design,
following an 1850s expansion
of the rest of the building.

◀ **Sewall-Belmont House:** *One of the oldest houses remaining in the District, the Sewall-Belmont House was built in 1800 (incorporating in part a 1680 structure) by Robert Sewall on land given to Lord Baltimore by King Charles II in 1632. Rebuilt in 1929, the house was then sold to the National Women's Party, of which Alva Belmont was a major benefactor. Today it is a museum to the women's rights movement, as well as headquarters of the current NWP.*

▼ **Supreme Court:** *One of the more imposing Federal buildings in Washington is situated across the street from the east side of the Capitol. The Supreme Court Building, which was actually completed in 1935, houses the courts of the nation's highest judicial tribunal. The plaza in front is occasionally the site of demonstrations related to cases under consideration within.*

▲ **Library of Congress Interior:** *What is now called the Jefferson Building of the Library of Congress was planned in 1871; construction began in 1886 and was completed in 1897. In spite of the building's quite lavish decorative details, it was* *completed for $200,000 less than the original appropriation of $6,500,000. Today, the Library houses more than 100 million items— including photographs, prints, audio recordings, and film— in three massive adjoining buildings plus offsite storage.*

▲ **Library of Congress:** *Founded as a legislative library to serve Congress in 1800 with the acquisition of 740 books from London, the Library of Congress has since become* *the de facto library of record in the United States, housing at least one copy of every work published in the U.S. The Jefferson Building, shown here, was planned to house three million works.*

▲ **Library of Congress Main Reading Room:** *An awe inspiring room described as being like the interior of a giant Fabergé egg.*

◀ **National Postal Museum:** *Across Massachusetts Avenue from Union Station, the National Capital Station Post Office served the postal needs of downtown Washington from 1914 until 1986. The lower level was reopened in 1993 as the National Postal Museum, a Smithsonian complex that depicts the history of the U.S. Postal Service over the years. The upper floor is host to a brewpub restaurant.*

▶ **Folger Shakespeare Library and Theatre:** *A reference library, an exhibition hall, and a theater reside in this marble Art Deco building on East Capitol Street, designed by Paul Philippe Cret and opened in 1932. The Folger Shakespeare Library and Theatre is dedicated not only to the works of William Shakespeare—it contains the world's largest collection of his printed works—but also to the literature and culture of the Elizabethan era.*

▲ **Union Station:**

Washington Union Terminal, or Union Station, was built in 1903–7 to consolidate the passenger operations of the major railroads then serving Washington. The building saw declining use in the later twentieth century, but in the 1980s it underwent a $160 million restoration and redevelopment as a successful commercial shopping center, neatly integrated into its role as an Amtrak intercity and commuter rail station.

◀ **Bartholdi Fountain:**
The designer of New York's Statue of Liberty, Frédéric-Auguste Bartholdi, also designed this cast-iron statue of three sea nymphs for the Centennial Exposition in 1876. It was relocated to this park at Independence Avenue and 1st Street SW in 1934.

▲ **U.S. Botanic Garden:** *A museum or "zoo" of living plants, oddly situated at the foot of Capitol Hill next to the Mall, the Botanic Garden occupies a building constructed to resemble London's iron-and-glass Crystal Palace of 1857. The Botanic Garden features rotating exhibits of plants and their interactions with nature and humankind, endangered or threatened plant species, desert and jungle landscapes, and a three-acre garden.*

Pennsylvania Avenue

Pennsylvania Avenue technically stretches from M Street in Georgetown all the way southeast to the District Heights suburbs and past the Beltway to Upper Marlboro, Maryland. But today, when people mention "Pennsylvania Avenue", they are referring in all probability only to the stretch between the White House and the Capitol. This 16-block boulevard is often considered in symbolic terms "America's Main Street." Without a doubt, that was the effect intended by L'Enfant in its design.

Though it now largely lacks the typical bustle and glitz of most such major avenues, including New York City's Broadway or Fifth Avenue, its symbolism has been enormously apparent for decades. All manner of parades, from Presidential inaugurations to protest marches and from wartime military processions to state funerals, have occurred on this avenue, and will probably do so for decades to come.

Over the past century, more federal buildings and monuments have been erected on the sites of former hotels, taverns, markets, and businesses, making the avenue increasingly majestic and less commercial in nature and appearance. Principal among the conversions was the Federal Triangle project of the 1920s and 1930s, which saw the demolition of large swaths of former commercial buildings to clear entire blocks for the buildings that would later house the expanding bureaucracy of the New Deal programs and post-World War II prosperity. Many of the more modern additions, such as the FBI Headquarters and the Canadian Embassy, made a dramatic change from the Classical styling of such buildings as the Department of Justice Building and the National Archives, but still only put a stark modern twist to the neighborhood. Thankfully, an injection of new life came about from a commercial redevelopment of the Old Post Office—the last of the older stone edifices from the older days—and the redevelopment of the old "downtown" 7th Street just north of Pennsylvania Avenue as a commercial strip.

On the west side of the White House, the most prominent landmark is George Washington University, lining the south side of Pennsylvania Avenue as it approaches Washington Circle and Foggy Bottom.

▶ **Old Post Office:** *Constructed in 1899 to serve as both the city's main post office (replaced by the one on page 40 in 1914) and as offices for the U.S. Post Office Department (which lasted until 1934), the Old Post Office was threatened with demolition several times until preservationists rallied to the cause of the building and it was renovated in 1978–83 for office and commercial use. The 315-foot clock tower—third-tallest landmark in the city—houses an observation deck open to the public.*

▶ **Market Square/U.S. Navy Memorial:** *Originally a market area, the plaza surrounding the area of Pennsylvania Avenue, 7th Street, and 8th Street NW is now home to several noted monuments, including the U.S. Navy Memorial and the Grand Army of the Republic Monument. The latter was erected in 1909 to commemorate the first veterans' organization in the United States, formed by veterans of the Union Army in the Civil War and instrumental in establishing Decoration Day (now known as Memorial Day) as a Federal holiday.*

◀ **Pennsylvania Avenue:** *The route connecting the Capitol and the White House—Pennsylvania Avenue—is more than just physical; it is also symbolic, and it is one of the nation's most noted boulevards. Both commercial and governmental buildings line the route, which is part of the Federal Triangle.*

▶ **FBI Headquarters:** *The J. Edgar Hoover Building of the Federal Bureau of Investigation, on E Street and Pennsylvania Avenue between 9th and 10th Streets, was opened in 1974. The design of the building stands in sharp contrast to the Classical architecture of the Federal Triangle district, and has been referred to as "neo-Brutalist" by its detractors.*

Tidal Basin & Constitution Gardens

The western half of the Mall, between the Washington Monument and the Lincoln Memorial, has a distinctly different character than the eastern half—considerably more park-like in nature with more greenery. It is, in effect, a garden of memorials and monuments, with little else in the neighborhood. To the south of the Mall in this area is the Tidal Basin, a small non-navigable harbor created in the 1890s by the Army Corps of Engineers to reduce the amount of stagnant water along the Potomac River and thus the incumbent risks of malaria and yellow fever.

Not long after its construction, travel writer Eliza Scidmore began planting cherry trees along the shores to beautify the otherwise barren Basin. The Japanese government began supplementing the trees with gifts of Japanese cherry trees, and by 1912, the Basin was liberally ringed with the trees. The annual blossoming of these cherry trees has become a much-loved springtime event, which is heralded with a Cherry Blossom Festival that draws hundreds of thousands of tourists every spring, crowding motels for miles around.

Other landmarks of the area include the Lincoln Memorial; the Reflecting Pool, which stretches between the Washington Monument and the Lincoln Memorial; the Constitution Gardens, commemorating the 56 signatories of the Declaration of Independence; the Vietnam Veterans Memorial within the park of the Constitution Gardens; and the Franklin Delano Roosevelt Memorial, completed in 1997. (Oddly, the FDR Memorial is the second such monument in the District; a simple block of stone, the size of Roosevelt's desk, sits in front of the National Archives, dedicated in 1965.)

Of all the monuments in Washington, D.C., the Vietnam Veterans Memorial is—even more than 20 years after its dedication—perhaps one of the most emotionally moving, as family members and friends scan the wall for the names of their fallen loved ones or comrades, which are engraved on the wall in the chronological order of their passings.

▶ **View West from the Top of Washington Monument:** *The scene to the west of the Washington Monument is dominated by the Lincoln Memorial and the Reflecting Pool, the latter patterned after similar pools at Versailles and the Taj Mahal. In the foreground is the new National World War II Memorial.*

▲ **Lincoln Memorial Interior:** *The epic 19-foot-high statue of a seated Lincoln, set to face the Reflecting Pool and the Mall, was sculpted by Daniel Chester French from 28 blocks of white Georgia marble. The surrounding walls are inscribed with quotations from Lincoln's Gettysburg Address and second inaugural speech.*

▶ **Lincoln Memorial:** *Constructed between 1914 and 1921 and dedicated in 1923, the Lincoln Memorial was designed by architect Henry Bacon based on a Greek temple design. The 36 columns represent the 36 states of the United States at the time of Lincoln's assassination in 1865.*

▲ **US Holocaust Memorial Museum:** Opened in 1993, the U.S. Holocaust Memorial Museum serves as a memorial to the millions who perished under Nazi rule in Germany and elsewhere in Europe between 1933 and 1945. The stark, industrial architecture is intended to be evocative of the themes of imprisonment and captivity that are documented within.

▲ **View South from the Top of Washington Monument:** *Seemingly no tourist visit to Washington, D.C. is complete without a climb to the top of the Washington Monument for its views of the city and surrounding areas—this one, looking south, shows the Tidal Basin and Jefferson Memorial. The tiny windows at the top afford spectacular vistas during clear weather.*

◀ **National World War II Memorial:** *Started in 1995 and dedicated in 2004, the National World War II Memorial honors all who served in the American armed forces during World War II. Although such a monument was overdue, its massive size and location— between the Washington Monument and the Reflecting Pool—created considerable controversy during its planning and construction and has led to calls for restrictions upon future building upon the Mall, lest it end up covered with monuments, like an overcrowded cemetery.*

◀ **Jefferson Memorial Interior:** *This memorial to the third President of the United States and primary author of the Declaration of Independence was begun in 1938 and dedicated in 1943. The circular dome, supported by 54 Ionic columns, houses a ten-foot bronze statue of Jefferson sculpted by Rudolph Evans, surrounded by panels inscribed with quotations from Jefferson's most noted writings.*

▲ **Jefferson Memorial and Tidal Basin:** *Adjacent to the Jefferson Memorial, the Tidal Basin was created in 1882 by the Army Corps of Engineers in an attempt to stem malaria and yellow-fever outbreaks associated with stagnant river lowlands. Shortly thereafter, writer Eliza Ruhamah Scidmore began planting cherry trees along its banks, and by 1912 the basin was ringed with thousands of them, many of which were a gift from Japan. The annual blossoming of the trees has become a major tourist draw and is the focus of an annual Cherry Blossom Festival.*

◀ **Korean War Veterans Memorial:** *Dedicated in 1995, the Korean War Veterans Memorial honors the approximately 1.5 million Americans who served in the "forgotten" Korean War of 1950–3. A series of 19 stainless-steel statues, designed by World War II veteran Frank Gaylord, is the central focus of the monument.*

▶ **Vietnam Veterans Memorial:** *Maya Lin's design for the Vietnam Veterans Memorial—a long wedge-shaped wall inscribed with the names of all 58,209 Americans who died in the Vietnam War—was originally criticized by many, but the acts by survivors of making a rubbing of a loved one's name as it appears on the monument or of leaving flowers or tokens in front of the names have become heart-touching daily rituals even years later.*

◀ **Franklin Delano Roosevelt Memorial:** *One of the newest monuments in Washington, D.C., dedicated in 1997, is the memorial to Franklin Delano Roosevelt, the nation's 32nd President and leader during World War II. The design by Lawrence Halperin resembles a sprawling park with waterfalls, granite walls inscribed with excerpts from FDR's speeches, and ten bronze sculptures lining the west side of the Tidal Basin.*

▲ **Bureau of Engraving and Printing:** *Sometimes referred to as the "money factory," the Bureau of Engraving and Printing is the printing plant for the nation's paper money, stamps, and bonds. Its tours and visitors center are popular with tourists young and old.*

▶ **Reflecting Pool:** *The concept of the Reflecting Pool, inspired by similar pools at Versailles and the Taj Mahal, originated with the McMillan Commission of 1902. It was originally intended to be cross-shaped, but temporary housing during World War I blocked the layout. The Pool typically freezes over during winter and becomes a popular skating venue.*

White House
& Foggy Bottom

This area is the location of arguably the most important address in the United States, the White House at 1600 Pennsylvania Avenue. It is also home to many notable (and associated) edifices, including the State Department, the U.S. Treasury Department, and the Old Executive Office Building, as well as the headquarters of the American Red Cross and the Organization of American States.

The White House itself remains one of the most popular attractions in the District, although it is increasingly difficult to tour in the wake of security threats. Many tourists content themselves with photographs from the outer fences, occasionally mingling with the ever-present token protestor or two on the Ellipse to the south or Lafayette Park to the north.

The neighborhood to the west and northwest of the White House owes its curious name to the former Potomac River swamplands, often foggy in the District's humid-yet-temperate climate, that were filled in to create the neighborhood's real estate. Among its landmarks is the complex that would inadvertently lend its name to the biggest American political scandal of the twentieth century—the Watergate office and residential complex bordering on Rock Creek Park. The Kennedy Center for the Performing Arts sits beside the Potomac as it turns north briefly toward Georgetown, buttressing the neighborhood like a majestic white river wall.

Foggy Bottom houses a large number of high-end apartment houses, tree-lined avenues, and elegant rowhouses, including some of the most valuable residential real estate in the nation. The neighborhood is also home to George Washington University, founded in 1821 in part to fulfill a vision of its namesake for a "national university" to be located in the nation's capital. It is now the largest university in the city.

▶ **White House:** *Located at the most famous address in the nation (1600 Pennsylvania Avenue), the White House is the oldest public building in Washington, D.C., albeit considerably altered from its original form. The design of the original structure was based on country-estate mansions in Britain and Ireland, but successive occupants have made a variety of changes to the house. Theodore Roosevelt officially renamed the edifice the White House in 1901.*

▲ **White House, Oval Office:** *The Oval Office is the official office space of the United States President, and is thus the symbolic center of American governmental leadership. The demands of modern technology and security have added features to the historical aspects of the office over the decades.*

▶ **Old Executive Office Building:** *Situated immediately to the west of the White House, The Old Executive Office Building was built between 1871 and 1888. Upon its completion, it was the largest office building in the world, with 566 rooms and close to ten acres of floor space. It originally housed the Department of War, and later the Department of State and the Navy.*

◀ **Willard Intercontinental Hotel:** *The most famous of Washington's classic hostelries, the Willard has long occupied the site of the original City Hotel, which was erected at 14th and Pennsylvania Avenue NW in 1816. The current structure, designed by Henry Hardenbergh (who also designed New York's Waldorf-Astoria and Plaza hotels), was erected in 1901. It closed in 1968 but was extensively renovated and reopened in 1986. It remains in service today as one of the nation's premier hotels, strategically located only three blocks from the White House.*

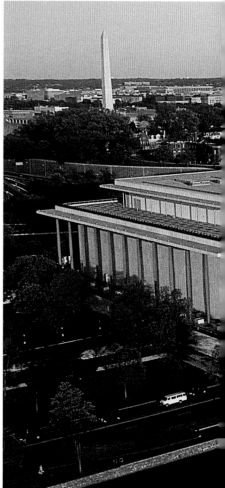

▶ **Kennedy Center for the Performing Arts:** *Opened in 1971, the Kennedy Center for the Performing Arts is also a symbolic memorial to President John F. Kennedy, assassinated in 1963. The center—a massive marble-clad structure along the banks of the Potomac River—houses six separate theaters for music, opera, cinema, and live theatre. It currently hosts around 3,000 performances a year to audiences in the millions.*

Blair House: *Across Pennsylvania Avenue from the White House, Blair House, built in 1858, is used as a guest house for foreign visitors and heads of state, and was even used as the Presidential residence by Harry S. Truman during the renovation of the White House. A guest bedroom is shown here.*

◀ **The Octagon House:** *Also known as the Dolley Madison House, the Octagon House was designed by William Thornton and built by John Tayloe III in 1799. Located at present-day 1741 New York Avenue NW, the house became the temporary residence of President James Madison and his wife Dolley after the burning of the White House by the British military in 1814. The building became the headquarters of the American Institute of Architects in 1899; a nonprofit arm of the AIA now operates the building as a museum.*

▶ **Lafayette Park:** *Located directly north of the White House, Lafayette Park honors the Marquis de Lafayette and other foreigners who aided the American cause during the American Revolution. Its proximity to the White House makes it a magnet for both tourists and protestors.*

▼ **Organization of American States:** *The group now known as the Organization of American States had its beginnings in 1890 as the International Union of American Republics, and later was known as the Pan American Union. Its current headquarters is located at 17th Street and Constitution Avenue NW, at the site of the Barnes House, one of the earliest houses in what would later become the District of Columbia, built in 1750 and demolished in 1894.*

▶ **Corcoran Gallery of Art:** *Washington's oldest art museum was originally located at the present-day Renwick Gallery; Corcoran's expanding collection relocated to this Beaux-Arts structure, designed by Ernest Flagg, in 1897. It is now the largest non-Federal arts museum in the District. A new wing, designed by Frank O. Gehry, was built in 1999–2003 to add another 110,000 square feet of display space.*

◀ **Watergate complex:**
This serpentine riverfront development of apartments and retail shops just to the north of the Kennedy Center had the misfortune to lend its name to the most notorious political scandal of twentieth-century America. In spite of this, the Watergate complex remains an upscale development today.

▲ **Department of the Interior:** *The otherwise nondescript Department of the Interior Building—a 1937 product of the Roosevelt building boom of the 1930s—features interior murals by Works Progress Administration artists of Indian life, national parks, and the pioneers' westward journeys, as well as a museum of Interior Department artifacts and artworks and Native American relics.*

◀ **Decatur House:** *Designed for War of 1812 naval hero Stephen Decatur by Benjamin Latrobe and built in 1819, the Federal-styled Decatur House is one of Washington's oldest surviving residential structures. It now functions as a museum exhibiting lifestyles of the city's elite during the early nineteenth century.*

▶ **Thomas Circle:**
The statue of Major General George H. Thomas that lent its name to Thomas Circle (at the junction of 14th St and New Hampshire Avenue) remains at the circle's center to this day.

▼ **U.S. Treasury Building:** *The third-oldest building still in use by a Federal agency in Washington, the U.S. Treasury Building at 1500 Pennsylvania Avenue NW, was designed by Robert Mills, who was appointed Federal architect by President Andrew Jackson in 1836 and who also designed the nearby Patent Office and General Post Office. Jackson personally chose the site in the District's first radical departure from the L'Enfant city plan.*

▲ **Renwick Gallery:**
Financier and philanthropist William Wilson Corcoran commissioned this building—designed by noted architect James Renwick, Jr., and dating to 1859—as an art gallery, which he donated to the city. The Corcoran Gallery, as it was originally known, was relocated to a new building (see pages 70–71) at 17th Street and New York Avenue in 1897; the original building is now known as the Renwick Gallery and is used by the Smithsonian to display exhibitions of American crafts.

Downtown & North

The original downtown district of Washington, D.C., between Constitution and Massachusetts Avenues and 3rd and 14th Streets NW, bears little resemblance to its original commercial district origins. Through the 1800s, the area was gradually built up with shops, hotels, restaurants, newspaper offices, residences, and theaters. (Among the latter, Ford's Theater gained somber notoriety as the assassination site of President Abraham Lincoln in 1865.) By the early twentieth century, the neighborhood was Washington's premier shopping and entertainment district, featuring department stores such as Hecht's and Woodward & Lothrop in addition to the long-standing small-business mix.

The 1930s development of Pennsylvania Avenue and the adjacent Federal Triangle as government buildings, however, started a period of gradual decline for the area, which was hastened even more by the concurrent and later exodus of the middle class to the suburbs of Virginia and Maryland and the resultant decline in downtown shopping. By the 1980s, much of the downtown resembled a retail ghost town, with vacant department stores and seedy discount stores all too common in many larger American city downtown districts of the era. Strategic redevelopment in the 1990s, including the construction of an indoor sports arena, a larger convention center to replace the original one, and the complete redevelopment of entire blocks of historic structures, have brought back a great deal of the former bustle and nightlife, and the development process continues today.

The area is also home to several of the earliest Federal office buildings, such as the United States Patent Office at 8th and F Streets, and the Pension Building on F and G between 4th and 5th Streets. Many of these buildings have found new lives after their original occupants moved on to other locations or were assimilated into other departments. The Pension Building, for example, has become a monument to architecture as the National Building Museum, and the Patent Office has been renovated into a pair of Smithsonian art galleries. Sadly, such adaptive reuse still awaits some of the larger commercial buildings of the past, including several larger department stores and their warehouses, which remain vacant or underutilized.

▶ **The Brewmaster's Castle:** *This 31-room Victorian brownstone at 1307 New Hampshire Avenue NW was built in 1892–94 for beer magnate Christian Heurich. In 1956 it became the headquarters and museum of the Historical Society of Washington, D.C., but in 2003, the mansion was sold back to the family-operated Heurich House Foundation, which has pledged to preserve the house and continue to operate it as a museum, known as the "Brewmaster's Castle" or the Christian Heurich House Museum.*

▲ **Ford's Theater:** The downtown Ford's Theater would become noted in history primarily for the tragedy that occurred within on April 14, 1865, when John Wilkes Booth assassinated President Abraham Lincoln as he watched a play from the Presidential Box. The theater was closed, and was later used as a warehouse before being preserved as a National Historic Site in 1993. Restored to its former glory, it is again used as a theater, as well as being a tourist site dedicated to the assassination.

▼ **Carnegie Library:**
*Built in 1902 at Mt. Vernon
Square, the Carnegie Public
Library, later the Central
Public Library, served as
Washington's main library
until 1972, when it became
the library of the University of*
*the District of Columbia. In
1998, the building became the
City Museum of Washington,
D.C., administered by the
Historical Society of
Washington D.C.,
but was closed in 2003 due
to low visitor numbers.*

Pennsylvania Quarter: *Pennsylvania Quarter was the old name for what became the heart of commercial downtown Washington during the nineteenth and twentieth centuries. Originally clustered shop buildings, the area later saw department stores and hotels before suffering a late-twentieth-century decline as businesses and shoppers fled to the suburbs. Recent redevelopment has injected new life into the area, with new shops and restaurants housed in the old buildings.*

MCI Center: *A 20,000-seat entertainment and sports arena, the MCI Center on 7th Street has effectively anchored the economic revival of the downtown district since its opening in 1997. It is home to the Washington Wizards and Mystics basketball teams and the Washington Capitals hockey team, as well as hosting all sorts of events from circuses to concerts.*

▲ **Chinatown:** In spite of Washington's Chinatown neighborhood being but a mere shadow of its former 1930s self, the Chinatown Friendship Archway, designed by Alfred Liu for the governments of Beijing and Washington, still spans the entrance to Chinatown at 7th and H Streets NW, directly adjacent to the MCI Center.

▶▶ **National Building Museum:** The spectacular building at 401 F Street NW, built in 1887 to a design by Montgomery C. Meigs, originally housed the Pension Bureau. Regarded as "Meigs' Old Red Barn" by early critics, and as a vacant eyesore in the 1960s, its renovation into a museum dedicated to architecture, engineering, and design was authorized by Congress in 1980.

◀ **Blaine Mansion:**
*This 1881 brick mansion
was home to James Blaine,
one of the founders of the
Republican Party. The
building, which is not open
to the public, blends a
curious mix of Victorian,
Gothic, Renaissance,
and Romanesque
architectural features.*

▲ **D.C. Convention
Center:** *The new
Washington, D.C. Convention
Center, on N Street between
7th and 9th St, opened in
2003, two blocks away from
the city's first convention
center (opened in 1983 and
since demolished). The center
hosts not only conventions,
but also public events such
as speeches and conferences
by visiting statesmen.*

Embassy Row & North

"Embassy Row" is the all-but-official name given to the stretch of Massachusetts Avenue between Scott Circle and the U.S. Naval Observatory. Though not every embassy in the city is located on this stretch, the diversity of flags to be seen here is reminiscent of a flag store or the United Nations. The gathering of embassies has its origins in the Great Depression of the 1930s, when formerly wealthy families who had lost substantially in the 1929 stock market crash were forced to sell off long-held mansions to any willing buyers, usually diplomats shopping for suitable housing for foreign missions. Since the original buying spree, more embassies have been purchased or built, usually in styling sympathetic to the street's majestic architectural gems.

Also a part of Embassy Row is Dupont Circle, which was on the outskirts of town in the early and mid-1800s. If any part of the District is to be thought of in terms of Broadway or Beverly Hills, this is it. The Dupont Circle neighborhood is a bustling cluster of upscale restaurants, bars, clubs, and boutiques, and the circle itself sports a fine park. (Oddly, two trolley tunnels once burrowed underneath Dupont Circle to speed streetcars through. Upon their abandon-ment, along with the trolleys, in 1962, the tunnels were pro-posed for subterranean commercial development several times. The only serious attempt, a food court, lasted but briefly in the 1990s.)

To the north of Dupont Circle and Embassy Row lies the Adams Morgan neighborhood, a lively and trendy multi-ethnic area that attracts a slightly younger demographic to its social and cultural scene. It, too, is filled with fine old brownstones and vintage apartment buildings, and the commercial strip of 18th Street is reminiscent of New York's City's Greenwich Village.

Further to the north, one finds Rock Creek Park, which occupies the valley formed by the stone-filled creek that runs from Maryland to the Potomac. Among the highlights of Rock Creek Park is the National Zoological Park, the Smithsonian-administered zoo. Further to the northwest, at the junctions of Massachusetts and Wisconsin Avenues and one of the highest points in the District, sits the Washington National Cathedral, constructed over most of the twentieth century and completed in 1990.

▶ **Embassy Row:** *The two-mile stretch of Massachusetts Avenue northwest between Scott Circle and Observatory Circle is popularly nicknamed "Embassy Row". The avenue is lined with spectacular mansions and residences from the nineteenth century, a great many of which over the years have been acquired by foreign nations for use as embassies and chancelleries.*

▲ **Washington National Cathedral Interior:** *The Washington National Cathedral hosts a seemingly endless schedule of daily worship services, tours, concerts, recitals, and other observances. Although the cathedral's principal architect is generally considered to be Philip Hubert Frohman, the building is in fact the product of the labor of untold hundreds of masons, architects, sculptors, and craftsmen.*

▶ **Washington National Cathedral:** *Construction on the cathedral—more formally called the Cathedral Church of St. Peter and Paul—began in 1907 and was essentially completed in 1990. The second largest cathedral in the U.S. and the sixth largest in the world, it functions as the main church of the Episcopal Diocese of Washington, and unofficially as the official-occasion church of the typically secular American government, open to those of all faiths.*

▶ **Pierce Mill, Rock Creek Park:** *A stretch of urban forest reaching along the aptly named Rock Creek from the Potomac River to the Maryland suburbs, Rock Creek Park was established by Congress in 1890. Its 1,755 acres encompass everything from horse and bike trails to a well-traveled parkway, and from this water-powered grain mill to a Civil War fort.*

▲ **Hillwood Museum and Gardens:** *Occupying a 40-room Georgian mansion on a 25-acre estate beside Rock Creek Park, the Hillwood* *Museum and Gardens display Russian and French decorative art from the collection of twentieth-century socialite Marjorie Merriweather Post.*

◀ Russian (ex-Soviet) Embassy: *The Russian Embassy sits separate from Embassy Row along Wisconsin Avenue next to the Glover Park neighborhood. It gained notoriety in its past life as the embassy for the Soviet Union, the "Cold War" enemy. So much diplomatic wireless communication flowed to and from the fortress-like compound that neighbors claimed difficulty in receiving local TV and radio broadcasts.*

◄ **American University:** *Located on 80 acres of upper Northwest Washington, American University is one of several universities in the city, with 11,000 undergraduate and graduate students. Other universities include Howard, George Mason, and Gallaudet Universities.*

▲ **Meridian House:** *The Meridian International Center was established in 1960 in two adjacent early 1900s mansions off 16th Street NW. The Center sponsors and facilitates international cultural exchanges; the mansions' ground floors are also open to the public, usually showing international art exhibitions.*

▲ ▶ **Dupont Circle:** At the junction of Massachusetts, New Hampshire, and Connecticut Avenues in northwestern Washington, Dupont Circle has long been the center of one of the city's most vibrant shopping, dining, and social districts. The circle originally sported a statue of Civil War admiral Samuel Francis Dupont (1803–65), erected in 1884, but the Dupont family later removed the statue to Wilmington, Delaware, and replaced it with a marble fountain by Daniel Chester French.

▼ **Panda House, National Zoological Park:** *The National Zoological Park opened in 1891 and has since become one of the world's finest zoos, housing more than 3,500 animals. The 163-acre complex, designed originally by Frederick Law Olmstead of New York's Central Park fame, is nestled between Connecticut Avenue and Rock Creek in the Cleveland Park neighborhood. Without a doubt the most popular exhibits here are the Chinese giant pandas.*

Georgetown

Georgetown is actually a relic of colonial times, predating the District proper. Originally the site of a Native American settlement, the area was part of a 1703 land grant to Ninian Beall, who named it "The Rock of Dumbarton". The community was renamed George in 1751 and incorporated as the City of Georgetown in 1789. Georgetown University—the oldest and largest Jesuit institution of higher learning in the nation—was also founded in 1789. Located along Georgetown's northwest corner, the university's large stone buildings now overlook Georgetown like a medieval castle on a rock.

By far the most historic and attractive of the neighborhoods of the District proper, Georgetown has developed over the years into a premier shopping and residential area, with scores of high-end retail outlets, several large estates and mansions, spacious brownstone rowhouses, and historical structures. Georgetown is also "high-society central," with jet-setters and the socially elite coming to see and be seen.

The present-day grandeur, however, belies the formerly industrial and gritty nature of the waterfront, which was lined with everything from stone-crushing plants to incinerators to a rendering factory. Much of this early industry arose here due to the proximity to the eastern terminus of the Chesapeake & Ohio Canal, the major transportation artery supplying the young District the coal, minerals, industrial products, and agricultural products of the markets and farms to the west, making Georgetown a commerce gateway to and from the developing American West.

Railroads, including a branch line from Silver Spring to Georgetown (now a bicycle trail) would render the canal largely redundant in the later nineteenth century, shifting some of the freight burden off Georgetown. Today, the remains of the C&O Canal are a Potomac-side footpath from the District to Cumberland, Maryland, but a restored segment of the canal is now refilled with river water every summer to offer vintage-style canal barge rides to tourists.

▶ **Georgetown houses:** *The real-estate listings might call the vintage and historical houses of Georgetown "quaint" or "charming," but there is no mistaking that many of the residences of the neighborhood qualify as some of the priciest in the nation.*

◀ **Chesapeake & Ohio Canal Mule Boats:** *The Chesapeake & Ohio Canal was begun in 1828 as a planned water transportation artery to connect Washington with the Ohio River and the American frontier, but the railroads rendered the canal largely obsolete before it could be pressed north or west out of Cumberland, Maryland, 185 canal miles to the west. A small segment of the eastern end is preserved in Georgetown with mule-pulled barges giving rides to tourists and history buffs.*

▶ **Wisconsin Avenue:** *Wisconsin Avenue stretches to the northwest from historic Georgetown, heading uphill toward the Glover Park and Mt. Alban neighborhoods and the Washington National Cathedral. Lined with shops and commercial buildings, it is progressively less upscale and more local in tone and market as it moves north.*

◀ **Commercial strip, M Street:** *Georgetown was incorporated into the District of Columbia in 1878. Since that time, it has prospered even further, becoming a very successful (and expensive) retail and residential district, combining both the charms of history and high-end commercial and restaurant trades. M Street, shown here, originally hosted taverns and shops that saw the likes of George Washington as visitors.*

◀ **Old Stone House:**
*Believed to be the oldest, if
not the only, colonial-era
structure surviving in the
District, Georgetown's Old
Stone House stands out
prominently among the more
contemporary commercial
and residential properties on
Georgetown's M Street. It now
serves as a museum and
visitors center operated by
the National Park Service,
with colonial-era furnishings.*

▲ **Georgetown
University:** *Founded in
1789, Georgetown University
was the first Catholic
university in the United States,
but it has welcomed those of
all faiths since its opening. It
now occupies 104 sylvan
acres and educates around
12,000 undergraduate and
graduate students annually.*

◄ **Dumbarton House:**
This brick Federal-styled house (not to be confused with the nearby Dumbarton Oaks) was built around 1800, relocated in 1915, and restored in 1928. Originally the home of Joseph Nourse, the first registrar of the Treasury, it is now operated by the National Society of the Colonial Dames of America as a headquarters and museum, containing period furnishings, china, silver, Persian rugs, and prints of the District.

► **Dumbarton Oaks:**
Dumbarton Oaks is maintained as a museum and garden by Harvard University, to which its past owners, Robert Bliss and his wife, bequeathed the building in 1940. It now houses a research center and a museum of Byzantine and pre-Columbian art, sculpture, jewelry, and textiles, along with a beautiful garden covering ten acres.

◄ **Washington Harbor:**
Located at 31st and K Streets NW, Washington Harbor is a combined commercial and residential waterfront development built in the 1980s atop a former industrial site and cement factory. The waterfront includes a wide river promenade and plaza, bicycle lanes, indoor and outdoor shops, and among the best views of the Potomac River in Washington.

East, South, & Southeast

By virtue of the geography of the District, the Northwest quadrant of the city is by far the largest. The regression of the former District lands on the south side of the Potomac back to the Commonwealth of Virginia in 1846 largely distorted the original four-way quartering of the District that was centered on the Capitol. A large proportion of the real estate to the southeast and east lies on the other side of the somewhat stagnant Anacostia River, which in the District is little more than an estuary into the Potomac (and for years was a highly polluted waterway).

Lining the shores of the Anacostia is an oddly eclectic assortment of military installations (such as Bolling Air Force Base and the Washington Navy Yard), and parks such as the Kenilworth Aquatic Gardens and a golf course. For the most part, however, the region lacks the huge diversity of tourist attractions of the rest of the region, and can almost be considered the "forgotten" part of the District, bisected in spirit by the Anacostia Freeway, which parallels the river and the southeastern District border.

A few attractions in the area and to the northeast of the Capitol are nonetheless worthy of the tourist's attention. Many of the sites relate to the long African-American heritage and history of the area; others, such as Fort Dupont Park, are associated with the Civil War defense of the city. The area is also home to Robert F. Kennedy Memorial Stadium—more frequently abbreviated "RFK Stadium"—built in 1961. The stadium was home to the Washington Redskins until 1997, when they moved to a new stadium in suburban Landover; it has also hosted professional soccer and concerts. In 2005 the stadium became the home of the new Washington Nationals Major League Baseball team, which is expected to spend at least the first couple of years at RFK until a new stadium deal or location is negotiated.

▶ **Basilica of the National Shrine of the Immaculate Conception:** *The Basilica of the National Shrine of the Immaculate Conception, on Michigan Avenue at 4th Street NE, is the largest Roman Catholic church in the United States, and one of the largest in the world. Its Byzantine and Roman-style architecture belies the fact that it was completed and dedicated in 1959. It can seat 2,500 and features more than 50 chapels dedicated to various visions of Mary.*

▲ **U.S. National Arboretum:** This 446-acre preserve in far northeastern Washington, founded in 1927, is dedicated to the conservation of and research on trees, as well as shrubs, flowers, and other plants from around the world. It also sponsors educational programs and demonstrations related to its missions.

▶ **Kenilworth Aquatic Gardens:** The Kenilworth Aquatic Gardens stands out as a wetlands alternative to the woods of the nearby Arboretum, with 14 acres of ponds and lush aquatic life, from water lilies to turtles and frogs.

Theodore Roosevelt Memorial, Theodore Roosevelt Island: *After Roosevelt's death on January 6, 1919, citizens wanted to establish a memorial in his honor, and the 91-acre wooded island in the Potomac seemed the perfect place to do so. The Theodore Roosevelt Memorial Association purchased the island in 1932. Congress approved funds in 1960, and the memorial was dedicated on October 27, 1967. The memorial was designed by Eric Gugler, the statue by Paul Manship.*

◀ **Frederick Douglass National Historic Site:**

Originally known as Cedar Hill, the beautifully restored 21-room home of Frederick Douglass, the former slave turned abolitionist and orator, sits across the Anacostia River from most of the District. Now maintained as a museum by the National Park Service, it preserves Douglass' personal library as well as many artifacts and Victorian furnishings.

◀ **Eastern Market:** *The oldest continuously operating fresh food market in the District, Eastern Market was designed by Adolph Cluss in the then-popular Italianate style and built in 1873. Inside, vendors offer fresh meats, flowers, eggs, produce, and baked goods. In spite of supermarkets and convenience stores opening since, it remains in operation as the last traditional market house in the District, though proposals to modernize its look and function are afloat.*

▶ **Fort McNair:** *Fort Lesley J. McNair, commonly called simply Fort McNair, has been the site of a military installation since 1791 when it was called Turkey Buzzard Point and later Greenleaf Point. The reservation has variously housed a fort, a federal penitentiary, and an army hospital; it is now home to the National Defense University. Fort McNair has housed the U.S. Army Military District of Washington headquarters since 1942.*

◀ **"The Awakening",**
Hains Point: *Located at Hains Point at the edge of East Potomac Park SW, "The Awakening," a sculpture by J. Seward Johnson Jr., depicts a giant 70-foot bearded man seemingly arising from the earth. The artist spent much of his career as a painter before moving to sculpture in 1968.*

Around Washington

The District of Columbia was a square patch of land spread across both Maryland and Virginia until 1846, when the portion of land on the Virginia side of the Potomac was ceded back to Virginia. For that reason, certain portions of the Virginia suburbs, including parts of Arlington and Alexandria, have over the years become closer to the District than they are to the rest of Virginia, both psychologically and physically. The Arlington National Cemetery, for example, is but one bridge across the Potomac apart from the Lincoln Memorial. Suburbs such as Herndon, Tysons Corner, and Falls Church now see business and retail traffic that would have been staggering to the old heart of the District.

The Maryland suburbs of the District, lacking the physical barrier of the Potomac River to separate them from the District, have long enjoyed a somewhat more homogenous relationship with their neighbor. Communities such as Glen Echo, Takoma Park, Bladensburg, and Suitland sprung up along the Maryland borders with the District, each to take a different role over the years. Some have remained quiet suburbs; others, such as Silver Spring and Rockville, have become economic centers in their own right.

As the population of the area has increased, along with the national population and the demands of an expanding government, the region has become a seemingly homogenous multi-jurisdictional region, with workers and shoppers increasingly commuting from suburb to suburb, city to suburb, and even from city to city. By 2000, the entire region from Baltimore, Maryland to Fredericksburg, Virginia and west to Frederick, Maryland was regarded by the U.S. Census Bureau as one massive metropolitan area—the fourth-largest in the nation, with a population of 7.6 million—though only 572,000 lived in the District proper, ranking it 21st among American cities. Transportation planners are now wrangling with the problems of how to reconfigure a transportation network designed around a central area (i.e. the downtown District) into a unified network serving a much broader area. Among the proposals are extensions of the Metro to Tysons Corner and Dulles Airport.

▶ **Freedom Park, Arlington:** *This small park in Arlington contains a monument to journalists killed in the line of duty and also artifacts relating to aspects of freedom, among them a section of the Berlin Wall, a toppled Lenin statue, and a South African ballot box.*

◄ **Arlington Memorial Bridge:** *Constructed between 1926 and 1932, the Arlington Memorial Bridge links the Lincoln Memorial and the entranceway to Arlington National Cemetery. Widely regarded as Washington's most beautiful bridge, the 2,163-foot bridge was originally constructed with a draw span in the center of the bridge, now inoperable and sealed shut.*

▶ **Arlington National Cemetery:** *The cemetery was created during the Civil War upon 200 acres of the estate of the Robert E. Lee family (inherited from his wife), seized for nonpayment of taxes during the war. It was then developed into a national cemetery for the war dead, and has continued to this day to be a repository for the remains of military service personnel, mostly those who have died in active duty.*

▶ **Pentagon:** *The physical and symbolic headquarters of the U.S. Department of Defense, the Pentagon was completed in 1943 after only 16 months of construction. It was, and remains, the world's largest office building, with 17 miles of hallways covering 34 acres and housing 23,000 military and civilian employees. Repairs to the building after a hijacked airplane crashed into it on September 11, 2001, were completed in months.*

◄ **Ronald Reagan Washington National Airport:** *Formerly called Washington National Airport, the airport across the Potomac from southernmost D.C. was renamed in 1998. Originally opened in 1941, this airport, the closest major airport to Washington, has been largely supplanted by Dulles International Airport in Virginia and Baltimore-Washington International Airport near Baltimore. A new 23-acre terminal building, designed by Cesar Pelli, was opened in 1997.*

▷ Iwo Jima Memorial, Arlington National Cemetery: *To the north of Arlington National Cemetery, the U.S. Marine Memorial, commonly known as the Iwo Jima Memorial, portrays in bronze the famous flag-raising on Iwo Jima in 1945 as captured on film by photographer Joe Rosenthal in one of the most iconic and famous photographs in history. The 32-foot-high figures support a 60-foot flagpole. The memorial was dedicated in 1954 after three years of construction.*

▷ George Washington Masonic National Memorial, Alexandria: *This 333-foot monument rising on Shooters Hill to the west of the original Alexandria was constructed by the Freemasons of America (of which Washington was a member) and dedicated in 1932, the 200th anniversary of his birth. The monument houses many artifacts of Washington's, including his family Bible and his Revolutionary War field trunk.*

Old Town Alexandria:
*Named for Scotsman John
Alexander, who purchased
much of what is present-day
Alexandria in 1669 from an
English ship captain for 6,000
pounds of tobacco, Alexandria
was incorporated in 1749
and served as a popular port
and commerce center until
overshadowed by the District
of Columbia. Today, Old Town
Alexandria still retains much
of its antique colonial charm,
deftly melded into the
demands of modern-day
commerce and tourism.*

**Christ Church,
Alexandria:** *Built by John
Carlyle, the founder of Arlington,
in 1773, this humble English
country-style church has been
in continuous use as an
Episcopal house of worship ever
since. It was the home parish
of both George Washington and
Robert E. Lee, and plaques
mark the location of their
chosen pews. The church is open
to visitors daily.*

**Gadsby's Tavern,
Alexandria:** *Comprising a
1770s tavern and a 1792
hotel along with other
outbuildings, Gadsby's Tavern
was a former business and
social center of the colonial and
early American Alexandria. It
has now been restored as both
a museum of early American life
and an operating restaurant.*

◄ **Mount Vernon Estate and Gardens:**
The Georgian-styled family mansion of George Washington sits on 500 acres of his Mount Vernon estate, which overlooks the Potomac south of Alexandria. The Mount Vernon Ladies Association purchased the estate for preservation from a Washington relative in 1858, and continues to own and operate the site as a historic home, museum, and garden estate.

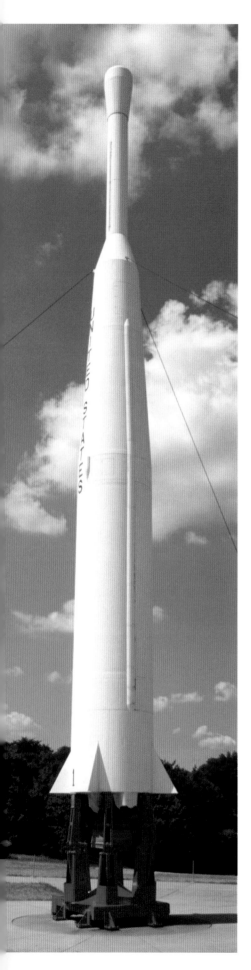

◄ **NASA Goddard Space Flight Visitors Center, Greenbelt:** *The Goddard Space Flight Center is the Washington-region command center of the National Aeronautical and Space Administration, which among other duties oversees satellites and space missions. The site's visitors' center explores the history of American rocketry and space programs, such as the flights to the moon, exploratory missions to other planets, and the Hubble Space Telescope.*

▲ **American Film Institute Silver Complex, Silver Spring:** *The American Film Institute, a membership association for movie enthusiasts, which was formerly headquartered in the Kennedy Center, has renovated the former Silver Theater on Colesville Road in Silver Spring, Maryland. The AFI Silver Theater opened in 2003 as an operating theater showing a broad spectrum of vintage, classic, avant-garde, and new films and programs on behalf of the AFI.*

▶ **Mormon Tabernacle:** *Properly known as the Temple of the Church of Jesus Christ of Latter-Day Saints, but popularly referred to as the Mormon Tabernacle, the spectacular six-spired structure, completed in 1974 at a cost of $15 million, is located in suburban Kensington, just outside of and beside the Beltway. Its grandiose appearance often prompts comparisons—favorable or unfavorable—to the appearance of The Emerald City in the classic movie The Wizard of Oz.*

▲ **Glen Echo Park:** *Glen Echo Park began in 1891 as a National Chataqua Assembly dedicated to the teaching of arts, sciences, literature, and languages. By the early 1900s, however, the park had evolved into an amusement park located at the rural end of a trolley line. The amusement park closed in 1968, and Glen Echo Park is now a historic park administered by Montgomery County and the National Park Service as a center for art, theatre, and dance.*

▶ **Great Falls, Potomac River:** *Located on the Potomac River several miles northwest of the District, Great Falls lacks the height or spectacle of Niagara Falls. Nonetheless, its proximity to the District, along with the adjacent county and national parks and the scenery, make this minor gorge a popular weekend destination for tourists. Kayakers in particular are attracted to the craggy whitewater rapids.*

Index

Washington, D.C., Map

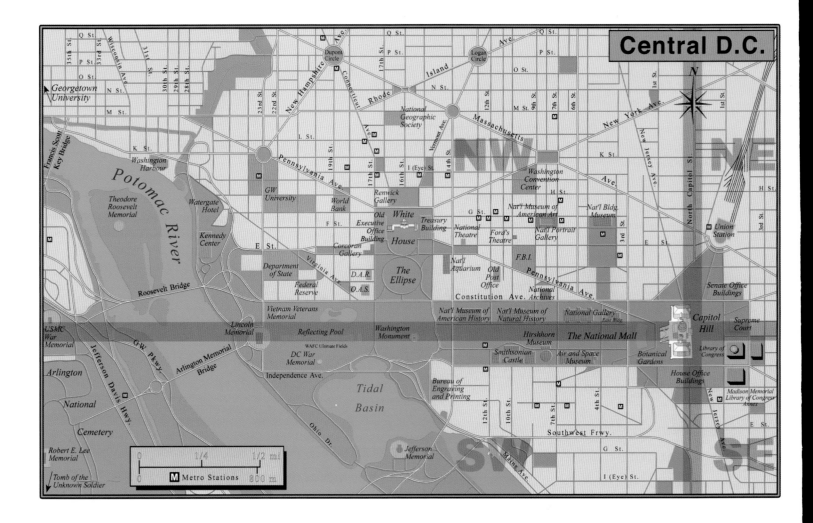